Table of Contents

Lesson 1
Galatians 1:1-6

This is the study of the book of Galatians which is an epistle or letter written by Paul. Have you ever studied the book of Galatians? Paul introduces himself as an apostle of our Lord and Savior, Jesus Christ and of God our Heavenly Father.

He is writing this letter to the churches of Galatia. The epistle is thought to have been written around 50 A.D. Notice the Scripture says churches. This letter wasn't written to one specific church, as many of Paul's writings were, but it was written to all the churches in the region of Galatia. Do you know who the people of Galatia were?

The region of Galatia was a Roman Province in Asia Minor. It was thought to be inhabited by Celtic people who were called Gauls. The name Galatia means land of the Galli or Gauls. There were two regions of Galatia a northern region, which was small agricultural cities, and the southern region, which was more commercial.

Paul starts with a greeting saying, "Grace and peace to you from God the Father, and from our Lord Jesus Christ. Who gave himself for our sins, that he might deliver us from this present evil world, according to the will of God and our Father: To whom is glory for ever and ever. Amen." If Paul considered the world to be evil at that time, what do you think he would think of our world today?

Paul made sure the churches of Galatia knew who he was representing when he wrote this letter. He had some things to discuss with them and he wanted them to know where he got his authority from so they would respect his writings. Paul was not called by man to be an apostle. His call to be an apostle was directly from God.

Paul's concern for the people of the churches of Galatia was that they had turned away from God and from the grace of Christ to another gospel so soon. When Paul started this chapter with the words grace and peace he knew that they couldn't have peace without the grace of God in their lives. They were called by God through Jesus to be His followers, but yet they turned away from Him. You can't turn to something else without first turning away from God.

Even though the people of Galatia lived long ago the messages Paul gives in the book of Galatians are messages and warnings for all of us. We need to be careful not to turn away from God, but to stay true to Him and His Word. In the next lesson we will look further into this matter and see how the churches of Galatia turned away from God and from the gospel of Jesus Christ. We will also see how Paul leads them back to God.

Daily Bible Scripture:

Galatians 1:1-6

1 Paul, an apostle, (not of men, neither by man, but by Jesus Christ, and God the Father, who raised him from the dead:)

2 And all the brethren which are with me, unto the churches of Galatia:

3 Grace be to you and peace from God the Father, and from our Lord Jesus Christ,

4 Who gave himself for our sins, that he might deliver us from this present evil world, according to the will of God and our Father:

5 To whom be glory for ever and ever. Amen.

6 I marvel that ye are so soon removed from him that called you into the grace of Christ unto another gospel:

Things to think about:

What did you learn about Paul and his dedication to the Lord in this lesson?

Who called Paul to serve the churches of his day?

What was Paul's concern for the people of Galatia?

Have you ever turned your back on God? What was the circumstance? What happened?

Prayer of the Day:

Dear Heavenly Father,

Thank You for this Scripture in the book of Galatians where we see that Paul was an apostle, called by You. It doesn't matter what other credentials he has. He had the highest calling and that was to be called by You to serve the churches of his day. Help us not to be worried about trying to impress men with our credentials, but to be more concerned about pleasing You. We see that Paul had a great concern for the churches of Galatia because they turned against You and against the gospel of the grace of Jesus Christ. Help us be on guard not to turn away from the gospel of Jesus Christ. In Jesus' name, we pray. Amen.

Paul Warns the Galatians
Lesson 2
Galatians 1:7-12

In this Scripture, we see Paul's concern for the people was legitimate. What was Paul concerned about in the previous lesson? Let's look at the Scripture in verse six and seven to see if we can find out why Paul was concerned. "I marvel that ye are so soon removed from him that called you into the grace of Christ unto another gospel: Which is not another, there are some that trouble you, and pervert the gospel of Christ."

Someone had brought "another gospel" to the Galatians. It was a perversion of the real gospel of Christ. He tells them that these people will cause trouble. They are trying to get the people of Galatia to believe something other than the true gospel which Paul preached to them.

The gospel of Christ may be hard for some people to believe, that Jesus came to earth as a man. He suffered and died in a gruesome way for our sins. He rose again on the third day. It may hurt some people's pride to know that they need a Savior. The fact that salvation is a gift of God and not something we can do for ourselves is hard for some people to accept. Have you accepted God's precious gift of salvation through His Son, Jesus Christ?

Paul tells them that if he, or anybody else - even an angel - preaches any other gospel to them except the gospel of the Lord Jesus Christ let them be cursed. Paul not only says this once, but twice. He shows his allegiance to the gospel of Christ.

Paul also talked to the Corinthians about this in 1Corinthians 15:1 when he said, "Moreover, brethren, I declare unto you the gospel which I preached unto you, which also ye have received, and wherein ye stand; By which also ye are saved, if ye keep in memory what I preached unto you, unless ye have believed in vain. For I delivered unto you first of all that which I also received, how that Christ died for our sins according to the scriptures; And that he was buried, and that he rose again the third day according to the scriptures..."

Paul tells the people that he is not trying to please men, but God, because if he tries to please men, how can he be a servant of Christ? He tells them that the gospel he preached to them wasn't of man, but he received the gospel by the revelation of Jesus Christ. Why would someone want to pervert the gospel of Christ?

In the next lesson we will see how Paul proves to the people that his message was from God.

Daily Bible Scripture:

Galatians 1:7-12

7 Which is not another; but there be some that trouble you, and would pervert the gospel of Christ.

8 But though we, or an angel from heaven, preach any other gospel unto you than that which we have preached unto you, let him be accursed.

9 As we said before, so say I now again, If any man preach any other gospel unto you than that ye have received, let him be accursed.

10 For do I now persuade men, or God? or do I seek to please men? for if I yet pleased men, I should not be the servant of Christ.

11 But I certify you, brethren, that the gospel which was preached of me is not after man.

12 For I neither received it of man, neither was I taught it, but by the revelation of Jesus Christ.

Things to think about:

What was Paul's concern in this Scripture?

Where did Paul say he received the gospel that he taught the Galatians?

Have you put your faith and trust in Jesus Christ?

What do you consider to be the gospel truth in your life?

Prayer of the Day:

Dear Heavenly Father,

Thank You for this Scripture in the book of Galatians where we see that Paul addressed the Galatians concerning their belief in "another gospel." Help us to study the Bible so we will know when someone is telling us the true gospel. Give us strength as we live in this world to share your gospel with others. In Jesus' precious name, we pray. Amen.

In His Time
Lesson 3
Galatians 1:13-24

We see in this Scripture that Paul acknowledges he persecuted the church in the past. Paul's persecution of the church of God is also spoken of in the book of Acts. Paul previously was very much into Judaism.

In God's perfect timing, He called Paul by His grace, to be an apostle and to preach the gospel of Jesus Christ to the heathen. When Paul was called by God he didn't go to the other apostles for their approval. He went straight to the lands of Arabia and Damascus to preach the gospel which God called him to do.

After three years of being in the ministry, Paul went to Jerusalem. There he met Peter and stayed with him for fifteen days. The only other apostle that Paul met at this time was James, Jesus' brother.

Paul swore before God that everything he was telling the Galatians was true. After Paul's visit to Jerusalem he went to Syria and Cilicia. Paul was unknown to the churches of Christ in Judaea. The only thing they knew about Paul was that he once persecuted the church of the Lord, but now he was preaching the gospel of the Lord Jesus Christ. The people glorified God for His work in Paul's life.

Isn't it amazing how God can take someone who was completely against God and His church, and turn that person completely around? He took Paul from being a persecutor of the church to preaching the gospel. Notice Paul says it happened in God's perfect timing, not in Paul's timing. Things don't always happen when we want them to happen, but they happen when God thinks the time is right.

Daily Bible Scripture:

Galatians 1:13-24

13 For ye have heard of my conversation in time past in the Jews' religion, how that beyond measure I persecuted the church of God, and wasted it:

14 And profited in the Jews' religion above many my equals in mine own nation, being more exceedingly zealous of the traditions of my fathers.

15 But when it pleased God, who separated me from my mother's womb, and called me by his grace,

16 To reveal his Son in me, that I might preach him among the heathen; immediately I conferred not with flesh and blood:

17 Neither went I up to Jerusalem to them which were apostles before me; but I went into Arabia, and returned again unto Damascus.

18 Then after three years I went up to Jerusalem to see Peter, and abode with him fifteen days.

19 But other of the apostles saw I none, save James the Lord's brother.

20 Now the things which I write unto you, behold, before God, I lie not.

21 Afterwards I came into the regions of Syria and Cilicia;

22 And was unknown by face unto the churches of Judaea which were in Christ:

23 But they had heard only, That he which persecuted us in times past now preacheth the faith which once he destroyed.

24 And they glorified God in me.

Things to think about:

> In what ways have you experienced God's perfect timing in your life?

> Does it amaze you how God transformed Paul's life?

> In what ways has God transformed your life?

> How have you surrendered your will to God's will?

Prayer of the day:

Dear Heavenly Father,
We thank You for this Scripture from the book of Galatians where Paul tells us about his conversion. He tells us that even though he was previously completely against the church You saved him and used him for Your glory. Help us to use Paul's testimony to realize there is hope for anybody. We see how You used Paul, in spite of his past, to spread the gospel. Help us to be willing to be used by You to spread the gospel in any way You see fit. In Jesus' name, we pray. Amen.

Paul Returns to Jerusalem
Lesson 4
Galatians 2:1-10

Paul tells us he went back to Jerusalem fourteen years later. After fourteen years why do you think Paul would return to Jerusalem? This time he took Barnabas and Titus with him.

Paul was called to preach the gospel of Christ to the Gentiles-anyone who was not Jewish. He was instructed by God to go to Jerusalem to share with them the gospel of Jesus Christ, which he had been preaching to the Gentiles. After the death of Jesus on the cross, the people of God were no longer under the law, but under the grace of God, through Jesus Christ. The people at Jerusalem believed that the Gentiles could be saved, but they believed that the Gentiles had to become Jews first.

Titus, who was a Greek, was not circumcised. He was Paul's missionary partner. Paul trusted Titus and knew that he had a heart for the gospel, just as Paul did. The people at Jerusalem were still living under the law and circumcision of the males was one of the requirements under the law of the Old Testament. It was a way for the Jewish people to show that they were set apart from others and were God's chosen people.

The only reason this question even came up was that there were false brethren who spied on Paul and his followers to see what liberties they had through grace and how they lived differently than the Jewish people. Paul, knowing that there were these differences in their beliefs met privately with the leaders to discuss their differences. The fact that Paul met with them privately and didn't dispute with them openly shows discretion on his part.

They saw that the same God that called Peter, who preached circumcision to the Jews, also called Paul, who preached uncircumcision to the Gentiles. James, Cephas (Peter), and John, who were their leaders in Jerusalem, saw the grace of God that was given to Paul.

Because of the laws of the Old Testament where the Jews were required to be circumcised a lot of times the Jewish people were considered to be the circumcision and the Gentiles were considered to be the un-circumcision.

Paul states in 1 Corinthians 7:18-20, "Is any man called being circumcised? let him not become uncircumcised. Is any called in uncircumcision? let him not be circumcised. Circumcision is nothing, and uncircumcision is nothing, but the keeping of the commandments of God. Let every man abide in the same calling wherein he was called."

Paul wasn't as concerned about people's outward appearance as he was about whether their heart was right with God. Sometimes we judge people by what we see on the outside and we can't see the work of God that may be going on inside of them.

They gave Paul and Barnabas the right hands of fellowship. They realized that Paul and Barnabas were called by God to preach salvation to the Gentiles, just as they had been called by God to preach to the Jewish people. The only thing the leaders of Jerusalem asked was for Paul to teach the other churches to remember the poor, which Paul already did.

Daily Bible Scripture:

Galatians 2:1-10

1 Then fourteen years after I went up again to Jerusalem with Barnabas, and took Titus with me also.

2 And I went up by revelation, and communicated unto them that gospel which I preach among the Gentiles, but privately to them which were of reputation, lest by any means I should run, or had run, in vain.

3 But neither Titus, who was with me, being a Greek, was compelled to be circumcised:

4 And that because of false brethren unawares brought in, who came in privily to spy out our liberty which we have in Christ Jesus, that they might bring us into bondage:

5 To whom we gave place by subjection, no, not for an hour; that the truth of the gospel might continue with you.

6 But of these who seemed to be somewhat, (whatsoever they were, it maketh no matter to me: God accepteth no man's person for they who seemed to be somewhat in conference added nothing to me:

7 But contrariwise, when they saw that the gospel of the uncircumcision was committed unto me, as the gospel of the circumcision was unto Peter;

8 (For he that wrought effectually in Peter to the apostleship of the circumcision, the same was mighty in me toward the Gentiles

9 And when James, Cephas, and John, who seemed to be pillars, perceived the grace that was given unto me, they gave to me and Barnabas the right hands of fellowship; that we should go unto the heathen, and they unto the circumcision.

10 Only they would that we should remember the poor; the same which I also was forward to do.

Things to think about:

What was the dispute in this Scripture?

Why did the people want Paul to remember the poor?

What does it mean to you to believe the Gospel of Jesus Christ?

Why would you consider listening to any other gospel?

Prayer of the Day:

Dear Heavenly Father,

Thank You for this Scripture in the book of Galatians where we see that Paul was called to preach to the Gentiles just as You called others to preach to the Jews. We thank You that through Your Son, Jesus Christ, You made a way that we all could become Christians. We also see that You call different people to do different things. Help us to be faithful to whatever it is You call us to do. In Jesus' name, we pray. Amen.

Did Christ Die in Vain
Lesson 5
Galatians 2:11-21

As we study the Bible, we see in this Scripture in the book of Galatians that Paul and Peter met face-to-face in Antioch. Why was Paul upset with Peter? Peter had at one time befriended the Gentiles who came to Christ. When certain Jewish people came around, Peter separated himself from the Gentiles because he was afraid of what the Jewish people might think of him. Have you ever treated someone differently when other people were around because you were afraid of what they might think?

Some of the other Jewish people followed Peter's example and disassociated with the Gentiles as well. Peter knew the Gentiles weren't required to come under the law. Even Barnabas, who was a trusted friend of Paul, was led astray by Peter's actions. Paul confronted Peter about the way he was treating the Gentiles. Paul asked Peter, if he was living like the Gentiles why was he trying to make the Gentiles conform to the ways of the Jewish people?

Paul tells them even the Jewish people know that they aren't justified by the works of the law, but by their faith in Jesus Christ. Nobody, whether Jew or Gentile, can be justified by the works of the law: the only way we can be forgiven of our sins and justified in the sight of God is through our faith in Jesus Christ.

I love Galatians 2:20 where Paul says, "I am crucified with Christ: nevertheless I live; yet not I, but Christ liveth in me: and the life which I now live in the flesh I live by the faith of the Son of God, who loved me, and gave himself for me." Paul is saying that when he became a Christian his old spirit was crucified with Christ. Even though he still lives in his body, now he has a new spirit because Christ lives in him. The life he lives in the flesh he lives by the faith of the Son of God, Jesus, who loved him and died for him.

Paul says that he doesn't discourage the grace of God: because if we receive our righteousness by obeying the law, then Christ died in vain. God knew that we wouldn't be able to keep the law, so He sent His Son, Jesus, to die on the cross for us so we might have a sacrifice for our sins.

It is by the grace of God through our faith in Jesus that we can become Christians. This is best described in Ephesians 2:8-9 which says, "For by grace are ye saved through faith; and that not of yourselves: it is the gift of God: Not of works, lest any man should boast."

Daily Bible Scripture:

Galatians 2:11-21

11 But when Peter was come to Antioch, I withstood him to the face, because he was to be blamed.

12 For before that certain came from James, he did eat with the Gentiles: but when they were come, he withdrew and separated himself, fearing them which were of the circumcision.

13 And the other Jews dissembled likewise with him; insomuch that Barnabas also was carried away with their dissimulation.

14 But when I saw that they walked not uprightly according to the truth of the gospel, I said unto Peter before them all, If thou, being a Jew, livest after the manner of Gentiles, and not as do the Jews, why compellest thou the Gentiles to live as do the Jews?

15 We who are Jews by nature, and not sinners of the Gentiles,

16 Knowing that a man is not justified by the works of the law, but by the faith of Jesus Christ, even we have believed in Jesus Christ, that we might be justified by the faith of Christ, and not by the works of the law: for by the works of the law shall no flesh be justified.

17 But if, while we seek to be justified by Christ, we ourselves also are found sinners, is therefore Christ the minister of sin? God forbid.

18 For if I build again the things which I destroyed, I make myself a transgressor.

19 For I through the law am dead to the law, that I might live unto God.

20 I am crucified with Christ: nevertheless I live; yet not I, but Christ liveth in me: and the life which I now live in the flesh I live by the faith of the Son of God, who loved me, and gave himself for me.

21 I do not frustrate the grace of God: for if righteousness come by the law, then Christ is dead in vain.

Things to think about:

Why was Paul upset with Peter?

What does it mean to have Christ living in you?

Is Christ living in you? If not, why?

Prayer of the Day:

Dear Heavenly Father,

We thank You for this Scripture in the book of Galatians where Paul defended the Gentiles. He knew that Your plan included the Gentiles. It includes all of us and for that we thank You. Thank You for sending Your Son, Jesus to die for our sins. Help us who have received Him as our Savior to live a life worthy of His sacrifice. Help those who haven't yet accepted Him see their need for the Savior. In Jesus' name, we pray. Amen.

Oh Foolish Galatians
Lesson 6
Galatians 3:1-5

In this Scripture, we see that Paul confronts the Galatians about their beliefs. Paul called them foolish and asked them who had bewitched them. What do you think Paul meant by that question? Paul was concerned because he knew that the Galatians knew right from wrong, but they let someone convince them of something which was not true. The Galatians were acting as if a spell had been cast on them.

Paul reminds them Jesus Christ was crucified before their eyes, yet they believed things that weren't true. Paul knew the Galatians were taught the gospel of Jesus Christ, the good news of salvation, but somehow they let someone deceive them. Paul asked them if they thought they received the Holy Spirit by the works of the law, by obeying all the rules perfectly or by hearing the gospel and receiving it by faith. Salvation is a gift from God to those who receive it and the promise of eternal life in heaven after this life is over. If someone gives you a gift, do you have to work for it? Do you receive it graciously?

Jesus says all we need to do is ASK: Matthew 7:7-11 says, "Ask, and it shall be given you; seek, and ye shall find; knock, and it shall be opened unto you: For every one that asketh receiveth; and he that seeketh findeth; and to him that knocketh it shall be opened. Or what man is there of you, whom if his son ask bread, will he give him a stone? Or if he ask a fish, will he give him a serpent? If ye then, being evil, know how to give good gifts unto your children, how much more shall your Father which is in heaven give good things to them that ask him?"

Paul asked the Galatians if they were so foolish to think that they began their relationship with Christ through the Holy Spirit, but now they think they can be made perfect by the works of the flesh. Sometimes we try to make things a lot more complicated than they are. We think somehow we can do something to earn what Jesus has already made available to us. Our relationship with Christ grows as our faith in Him grows.

Paul asks the Galatians if they had suffered in vain. In the book of Acts there are accounts of Paul being persecuted for preaching the gospel of Christ. If he was persecuted, it is probable that the churches of Galatia were persecuted also. If they didn't believe the gospel had to be received by faith, then their suffering was in vain.

Paul asks them, "If He who ministers to you by the Spirit, and works miracles among you, does He do it by the works of the law, or by the hearing of faith?" Paul is speaking of God. Miracles are received through faith. He is the one who gives Christians the gift of the Holy Spirit when they receive Christ through faith.

Our Triune God doesn't leave us or forsake us. When Jesus Christ ascended to heaven He sent the Holy Spirit to be our comforter and guide.

As Christians we need to study the Bible for ourselves and know what it says so we won't be lead astray.

Daily Bible Scripture:

Galatians 3:1-5

1 O foolish Galatians, who hath bewitched you, that ye should not obey the truth, before whose eyes Jesus Christ hath been evidently set forth, crucified among you?

2 This only would I learn of you, Received ye the Spirit by the works of the law, or by the hearing of faith?

3 Are ye so foolish? having begun in the Spirit, are ye now made perfect by the flesh?

4 Have ye suffered so many things in vain? if it be yet in vain.

5 He therefore that ministereth to you the Spirit, and worketh miracles among you, doeth he it by the works of the law, or by the hearing of faith?

Things to think about:

What was Paul's concern with the Galatians in this Scripture?

Is your faith and hope in Jesus Christ? If not, why? If so, how are you certain?

How does the Bible say we are saved?

Prayer of the Day:

Dear Heavenly Father,

We thank You for this Scripture in the book of Galatians where Paul talks to the Galatians about the difference in the works of the law and in faith in Christ. As Christians we have to remember that Christ took our place and took our sins upon Him so through faith we can be saved from our sins. There is nothing we can do to save ourselves except to believe in Him. Help us Lord to get a grasp of this and not make serving You complicated. Help us to study the Bible so we will know what the truth is and can live our lives according to the truth. In Jesus' name, we pray. Amen.

Abraham Believed God
Lesson 7
Galatians 3:6-14

We see in this Scripture that Paul speaks to the churches of Galatia about Abraham. What did Abraham have to do with the churches of Galatia?

Paul tells them that Abraham's righteousness was accounted to him because Abraham believed God. He didn't just believe there was a god. When the Scripture says Abraham believed God it means he trusted and had complete faith in God. Abraham believed the promise that God made to him.

Abraham was promised by God when God appeared to Abraham in Genesis 17:1-5 that all nations would be blessed.

1 And when Abram was ninety years old and nine, the LORD appeared to Abram, and said unto him, I am the Almighty God; walk before me, and be thou perfect.

2 And I will make my covenant between me and thee, and will multiply thee exceedingly.

3 And Abram fell on his face: and God talked with him, saying,

4 As for me, behold, my covenant is with thee, and thou shalt be a father of many nations.

5 Neither shall thy name any more be called Abram, but thy name shall be Abraham; for a father of many nations have I made thee.

Man was not able to keep the law and the Scripture says that every man who breaks the law of God is cursed. Therefore, man is not justified by the law in the sight of God, but can only be justified by faith through Jesus Christ.

I once heard someone say that justified means just if I had never sinned. When Jesus covers your sin with His blood, God sees you just as if you had never sinned. We were redeemed from the curse of the law by Christ. Jesus was made a curse for us by being hanged on the cross. We no longer had to be under the bondage of trying to keep the laws of the Old Testament, because Jesus redeemed us when He took the punishment for our sins.

Jesus' death on the cross was orchestrated by God so that the Gentiles through Jesus might receive the blessing of Abraham and the promise of the Holy Spirit through faith as stated in this Scripture in Romans 11:25, "For I would not, brethren, that ye should be ignorant of this mystery, lest ye should be wise in your own conceits; that blindness in part is happened to Israel, until the fulness of the Gentiles be come in."

Our faith is not in Abraham, but our faith is in God through Jesus Christ. Look at this Scripture in Matthew 3:9, "And think not to say within yourselves, We have Abraham to our father: for I say unto you, that God is able of these stones to raise up children unto Abraham."

The Apostle Paul is trying to tell the Galatians not to rely on the fact that they were Jews and the descendants of Abraham; what is important is their faith in Jesus. By the same principle we can't rely on the belief that if we were born and raised in a Christian family we will automatically get to go to heaven. We all must have our own faith in God. It is an individual thing; nobody else can have faith for you. It is imperative that you have your own faith. You must accept Jesus Christ as your Savior. Nobody else can do it for you. It's a personal decision.

Daily Bible Scripture:

Galatians 3:6-14

6 Even as Abraham believed God, and it was accounted to him for righteousness.

7 Know ye therefore that they which are of faith, the same are the children of Abraham.

8 And the scripture, foreseeing that God would justify the heathen through faith, preached before the gospel unto Abraham, saying, In thee shall all nations be blessed.

9 So then they which be of faith are blessed with faithful Abraham.

10 For as many as are of the works of the law are under the curse: for it is written, Cursed is every one that continueth not in all things which are written in the book of the law to do them.

11 But that no man is justified by the law in the sight of God, it is evident: for, The just shall live by faith.

12 And the law is not of faith: but, The man that doeth them shall live in them.

13 Christ hath redeemed us from the curse of the law, being made a curse for us: for it is written, Cursed is every one that hangeth on a tree:

14 That the blessing of Abraham might come on the Gentiles through Jesus Christ; that we might receive the promise of the Spirit through faith.

Things to think about:

Do you believe God like Abraham did? Why or why not?

What was the promise God made to Abraham?

How did Jesus fulfill the law?

Prayer of the Day:

Dear Heavenly Father,

Thank You for this Scripture in the book of Galatians where Paul continues to explain to the churches of Galatia about faith. Help us as we study this Scripture to understand what the gospel of Jesus Christ is all about. Help us to put our faith in You and Your Son, Jesus Christ, and not in man. Help us to continue to study our Bible so we will know the truth of the gospel. In Jesus' name, we pray. Amen.

God's Promise to Abraham
Lesson 8
Galatians 3:15-20

We see in this Scripture in the book of Galatians that Paul continues to talk to the churches of Galatia about the law and faith. Paul tells the brethren that the promise God made to Abraham which we studied about in the previous lesson, is irrevocable. Nobody can do away with it or add to it. It was a promise between God and Abraham to be handed down throughout the generations to come.

God didn't say the promise was to Abraham and his seeds, but he said it was to his seed, which is one particular descendent of Abraham: Jesus Christ. This covenant was not only made with Abraham, but it was also made with Christ. The covenant that God made to Abraham four hundred and thirty years prior to God giving the law to Moses couldn't be annulled by the law.

If the inheritance is received by keeping the law, then it wouldn't be the result of the promise, but instead would be determined by our ability to keep the entire law or not. Paul asks them what the purpose of the law is. The law was added, or given to people to follow, because of our disobedience. The law was given to show us what God's standard was. Because God's standard is so high and man is sinful it also shows us our need for the Savior. The law was sent to man until the coming of the Savior.

Jesus wasn't sent to this earth by God to die on the cross in order to destroy the law, but His purpose was to fulfill the law, as mentioned in Matthew 5:17, "Think not that I am come to destroy the law, or the prophets: I am not come to destroy, but to fulfil."

Therefore, the keeping of the Law of Moses is no longer how we gain access to God. We come to God through faith in Jesus Christ. The law was given to Moses by angels; they were his mediator. We can go directly to God through Jesus, who is our mediator with God.

Jesus dying on the cross doesn't give us a permission to do as we please. We still must act responsibly and treat each other and God with respect. We do this as a way of honoring God and acting out our faith, not because we think that obeying all the rules gets us to heaven.

Daily Bible Scripture:

Galatians 3-15-20

15 Brethren, I speak after the manner of men; Though it be but a man's covenant, yet if it be confirmed, no man disannulleth, or addeth thereto.

16 Now to Abraham and his seed were the promises made. He saith not, And to seeds, as of many; but as of one, And to thy seed, which is Christ.

17 And this I say, that the covenant, that was confirmed before of God in Christ, the law, which was four hundred and thirty years after, cannot disannul, that it should make the promise of none effect.

18 For if the inheritance be of the law, it is no more of promise: but God gave it to Abraham by promise.

19 Wherefore then serveth the law? It was added because of transgressions, till the seed should come to whom the promise was made; and it was ordained by angels in the hand of a mediator.

20 Now a mediator is not a mediator of one, but God is one.

Things to think about:

To who was the covenant made?

Who is considered to be the seed of Abraham?

What was the promise that God gave to Abraham?

How does this promise apply to us today?

Prayer of the Day:

Dear Heavenly Father,

Thank You for this Scripture in the book of Galatians where Paul talks to the churches at Galatia about the promise to Abraham. Help us to see how it still applies to us today. Speak to the hearts of those who haven't yet accepted the promise. Help us to continue to study the Bible to learn about You and grow a deeper, more intimate, relationship with You through Your Son, Jesus Christ. In Jesus' name, we pray. Amen.

The Law Was Our Schoolmaster
Lesson 9
Galatians 3:21-29

We see in this Scripture in the book of Galatians that Paul asks an important question. Paul asks, "Is the law against the promises of God?" Paul says, "God forbid: if the law could have given life, then righteousness would have been by the law."

The law with all the rules and regulations of the Old Testament was given to tell us how to live, but being the sinful creatures that we are, we couldn't keep the law. The law was dependent on man's ability to keep it, which we failed at miserably. However, the promise of God through Jesus Christ (eternal life in heaven) isn't dependent on our ability to hold onto God through Jesus, but is God's promise to hold onto us for eternity through our belief in Jesus Christ.

Before faith came we were kept under the law. The law was our schoolmaster to bring us to faith in Christ that we might be justified, or forgiven of our sins, by faith. The law shows us that we are in bondage to our sin and we need the faith in Jesus to free us from that bondage. After faith came, we were no longer under bondage by the schoolmaster of the law. We are made children of God, or His heirs, by faith in Jesus Christ, which we will discuss more fully in the next lesson.

The idea that Paul uses a schoolmaster reminds me of when I was a child and was under the leadership of my teachers. They made the rules and if I didn't follow those rules I suffered the consequences. For most of you, your parents, or other adults in your life, not only taught you right from wrong, they took care of you, provided for you and protected you.

As you became an adult you remembered and respected what you were taught, but when you got out on your own you were no longer under their rule. They trusted you to do the right thing and to make right decisions based on what they had taught you over the years. The lessons they taught were meant to be carried with you for the rest of your life. The law was to teach, protect, provide, and correct Christians until the faith of Christ was revealed.

The law was God's way of protecting man until the coming of grace by Jesus' death on the cross. It gave Christians a model to live by. It shows us what kind of standards God has. The law kept man under its guard until faith was revealed. Just because we have Jesus in our lives doesn't mean we shouldn't try to live right. Faith doesn't give us a free ticket to do as we please.

Paul says those who've been baptized into Christ have put on Christ. This isn't talking about the water baptism that we think about when we say we've been baptized. Think of the picture of baptism. You are completely immersed in the water. When you put your faith in Christ you are baptized with Christ you are immersed with Jesus. He is a part of every aspect of your life.

My favorite verse from this passage of Scripture is Galatians 3:28 which says, "There is neither Jew nor Greek, there is neither bond nor free, there is neither male nor female: for ye are all one in Christ Jesus." Sometimes as humans we have our prejudices and think we may be better than someone else because of the color of our skin or our social status. This Scripture lets us know that as Christians we're all one in Jesus Christ. Paul tells us if we belong to Christ, then we are Abraham's seed, and heirs of the promise of God.

Daily Bible Scripture:

Galatians 3:21-29

21 Is the law then against the promises of God? God forbid: for if there had been a law given which could have given life, verily righteousness should have been by the law.

22 But the scripture hath concluded all under sin, that the promise by faith of Jesus Christ might be given to them that believe.

23 But before faith came, we were kept under the law, shut up unto the faith which should afterwards be revealed.

24 Wherefore the law was our schoolmaster to bring us unto Christ, that we might be justified by faith.

25 But after that faith is come, we are no longer under a schoolmaster.

26 For ye are all the children of God by faith in Christ Jesus.

27 For as many of you as have been baptized into Christ have put on Christ.

28 There is neither Jew nor Greek, there is neither bond nor free, there is neither male nor female: for ye are all one in Christ Jesus.

29 And if ye be Christ's, then are ye Abraham's seed, and heirs according to the promise.

Things to think about:

What was the purpose of the law?

What happened to the law after Christ's death on the cross?

How do we become God's children?

Prayer of the Day:

Dear Heavenly Father,

We thank You for this Scripture in the book of Galatians where Paul explains what it means to have faith in Christ. Even though the law is still today a good schoolmaster for us to learn Your ways and Your desires for our lives, we are so thankful for Your gift of faith to us. Help those who haven't put their faith and trust in Christ to realize their need for a Savior. Help those of us who've put our faith in Christ to stay true to our faith and continue to walk in it every day. In Jesus' name, we pray. Amen.

Why Live in Bondage
Lesson 10
Galatians 4:1-11

Paul talks to the churches of Galatia about being heirs of God. What does it mean to be heirs of God? Is being an heir the same as being a child or a servant?

In Greek, Hebrew, and Roman homes, minor children weren't considered an heir until they became a certain age or until the father decided that they were ready. When the heir was a child, he was no different than a servant, even though he was destined to be an heir. He was still under tutors and authorities until the father's appointed time when he would adopt him as an heir.

Paul was a Roman and their custom was for the father to decide when the child was mature enough to become an heir. First Corinthians 13:11 says, "When I was a child, I spake as a child, I understood as a child, I thought as a child: but when I became a man, I put away childish things." Paul now compares the child's bondage to the Christians bondage under the law.

My favorite verses in this Scripture are Galatians 4:4-5. Paul tells them, in the fullness of time, God sent His Son, made of a woman, made under the law, to redeem those that are under the law, that we might be adopted as sons. When you become a child of God, God sends the Spirit of His Son, Jesus, into your heart. You are no more a servant, but a child of God and an heir of God through Jesus Christ.

In Romans 8:14-17 the same idea of being freed from bondage and becoming an heir with Christ through the Spirit of adoption is stated:

14 For as many as are led by the Spirit of God, they are the sons of God.

15 For ye have not received the spirit of bondage again to fear; but ye have received the Spirit of adoption, whereby we cry, Abba, Father.

16 The Spirit itself beareth witness with our spirit, that we are the children of God:

17 And if children, then heirs; heirs of God, and joint-heirs with Christ; if so be that we suffer with him, that we may be also glorified together.

Paul asks the Galatians, how was it that when they didn't know God they served those who weren't gods. Paul couldn't understand, after they knew God and His freedom from all the rules and regulations of the Old Testament law, how they could turn back to the bondage of being under the law. Paul asks them, if they desired to be in bondage. He notes how they observe certain days, months, times, and years. Paul says he is afraid he has taught the Galatians to labor in vain.

Christ came to free us from the bondage of the law. These Christians were trying to put themselves back under the law. Paul is asking them, why they would want to be under the law, when Christ died to free them from that bondage.

Do we do that today, instead of living in the mercy and grace of God; do we put ourselves in bondage because of something we've done that was against the Law of Moses? If you are in Christ, you've been set free from bondage. Live in the freedom of grace and mercy that Jesus Christ died to give you.

Daily Bible Scripture:

Galatians 4:1-11

1 Now I say, That the heir, as long as he is a child, differeth nothing from a servant, though he be lord of all;

2 But is under tutors and governors until the time appointed of the father.

3 Even so we, when we were children, were in bondage under the elements of the world:

4 But when the fulness of the time was come, God sent forth his Son, made of a woman, made under the law,

5 To redeem them that were under the law, that we might receive the adoption of sons.

6 And because ye are sons, God hath sent forth the Spirit of his Son into your hearts, crying, Abba, Father.

7 Wherefore thou art no more a servant, but a son; and if a son, then an heir of God through Christ.

8 Howbeit then, when ye knew not God, ye did service unto them which by nature are no gods.

9 But now, after that ye have known God, or rather are known of God, how turn ye again to the weak and beggarly elements, whereunto ye desire again to be in bondage?

10 Ye observe days, and months, and times, and years.

11 I am afraid of you, lest I have bestowed upon you labour in vain.

Things to think about:

Why do we put ourselves in bondage when we can be free?

What does the bondage of sin do to us?

Since Jesus died to free us from bondage, what do we need to do to accept that freedom?

Have you been adopted into the family of God? If not, what are you waiting for? If yes, share the experience.

Prayer of the Day:

Dear Heavenly Father,

We thank You for this Scripture in the book of Galatians where Paul tells the Galatians that they no longer have to live under the bondage of the law, but as heirs of Christ they can live in grace and mercy. Help us to accept the grace and mercy that You provided for us when You sent Your Son, Jesus, to give His life on the cross for our freedom. Help us not to put ourselves in bondage under the law but to live as children of God, heirs of God, and joint heirs with Christ. In Jesus' name, we pray. Amen.

Be As I Am
Lesson 11
Galatians 4:12-20

As Paul continued to write his letter to the churches of Galatia He addressed his brethren, almost begging them, and saying, "Be as I am." Why would Paul say to the Galatians "Be as I am?" Wasn't Paul trying to point these people to Christ? Could you say to someone "Be as I am?"

Paul was walking in the freedom of Christ, not in the bondage of the law. He wanted the Galatians to walk in that same freedom. They'd been taught about the freedom they could have in Christ, but they'd let other people persuade them to go back to living under the law and trying to obey all the laws that were established in the Old Testament before Jesus Christ gave His life in remission for our sins.

You can tell in this portion of Paul's letter that he loved the Galatians. He'd been a part of them before, when he was there preaching to them. He had a heart for them and he wanted them to be free.

Paul says, "You know how I preached the gospel to you even though I had ill-health. You didn't reject me because of my thorn in my flesh, but you received me as a messenger of God, just like you would have treated Jesus Christ himself." Paul also speaks of having a thorn in the flesh in Corinthians. There is a lot of speculation about what Paul's physical ailment was, but nobody really knows.

Paul remembers that they would've done anything for him, even plucked out their eyes and given them to him if it was possible. Now that Paul was telling them the truth, he wondered if they would consider him to be their enemy.

Paul warns the Galatians that those people who wanted everyone to be legalistic were trying to influence them so they would follow them. They were trying to draw the Galatians away from the freedom they have in Christ and exclude them from the other Christians. But Paul wants the Galatians to be passionate about serving Christ always and not just when he is there with them. Paul knows they could have zeal for things that were good or bad, but warns them that it is dangerous to have zeal for things which are wrong.

Paul calls the Galatians, "my little children." This shows his love for them. Paul compares himself to a woman giving birth, saying he is travailing in birth again until Christ is formed in them. Paul thought he had birthed the Galatians into the family of God when he'd been with them before, but now that this situation came up, he felt like he needed to bring them to Christ all over again. Paul wished he could be with the Galatians because he had great concern for them and doubted they were on the right path he'd set them on. He wanted the best for the Galatians.

As a minister of the gospel, God had given Paul a great love, compassion, and concern for the people he had ministered to. In this Scripture you can hear the love, compassion, and concern in Paul's writing. He is concerned that the people he'd led to the Lord earlier were being led astray.

Paul wasn't trying to influence the people to be his followers, but wanted them to have a strong desire for following Christ and to live in the freedom that Christ died for them to have. Are you passionate about following Christ? Have you accepted the freedom of Christ in your life or are you still trying to keep the law?

Daily Bible Scripture:

Galatians 4:12-20

12 Brethren, I beseech you, be as I am; for I am as ye are: ye have not injured me at all.

13 Ye know how through infirmity of the flesh I preached the gospel unto you at the first.

14 And my temptation which was in my flesh ye despised not, nor rejected; but received me as an angel of God, even as Christ Jesus.

15 Where is then the blessedness ye spake of? for I bear you record, that, if it had been possible, ye would have plucked out your own eyes, and have given them to me.

16 Am I therefore become your enemy, because I tell you the truth?

17 They zealously affect you, but not well; yea, they would exclude you, that ye might affect them.

18 But it is good to be zealously affected always in a good thing, and not only when I am present with you.

19 My little children, of whom I travail in birth again until Christ be formed in you,

20 I desire to be present with you now, and to change my voice; for I stand in doubt of you.

Things to think about:

What did Paul mean by saying, "Be like me?"

What would give you the right to tell someone to be like you?

What does it mean to you to be passionate about following Christ and sharing the gospel with others?

Prayer of the Day:
Dear Heavenly Father,

Thank You for this Scripture in the book of Galatians where we see Paul's true love and concern for the Galatians. Help us to be zealous about following Christ and living in the freedom He died to give us. Help us to be zealous about sharing the gospel of Christ with others. Help us to be on guard against those who might try to lead us astray. Thank You for the pastors, teachers, and leaders that You send into our lives to lead us to You. In Jesus' name, we pray. Amen.

The Children of Promise
Lesson 12
Galatians 4:21-31

As we continue in the book of Galatians with the letter that Paul wrote to the Galatians. Paul inquires of them asking, "Those of you who desire to be under the law, do you not hear the law?"

Under the law, it is what you do, the rules you follow, that makes you right with God, but under grace it is what God did through His Son, Jesus Christ that makes us right with God. If you fail under the law, you are out of fellowship with God, but through grace and faith you can be forgiven.

Paul compares the law and faith to the difference between Abraham's two sons. Paul says, "It is written, that Abraham had two sons, one by a bondmaid and the other by a freewoman. Abraham's son Ishmael who was born of a bondwoman, was born of the flesh, but his son Isaac, who was born of the freewoman, was born by the promise."

If you remember in Genesis Sarah was barren for many years so she gave her handmaiden Hagar to Abraham who bore him a son called Ishmael. Sarah was impatient and tried to fix the problem on her own, but in God's time Sarah gave birth to Isaac, who was the son God promised her.

Paul talks about the two covenants and compares them. Paul says that Hagar is Mount Sinai in Arabia, the same mount where Moses received the law, answers to Jerusalem which is now in bondage with her children. However, Jerusalem above, which is Sarah is free, and is the mother above us all. Paul is speaking of the New Jerusalem.

Paul says, "It is written, rejoice those of you who are barren, cry out those of you that are not giving birth, the desolate have many more children than she which has a husband." Paul was saying that there would be more people born of the flesh than Christians, who are born of the promise.

Paul says that, we are like Sarah's son Isaac, the children of promise. Like Isaac those who are born of the promise will be persecuted by those who are born of the flesh. Paul reminds them that the Scripture says to cast out the bondwoman (Hagar) and her son (Ishmael). The son of the bondwoman won't be an heir with the son of the freewoman(Sarah). Likewise, we aren't sons of the bondwoman, but of the free.

Do you get the picture of how Paul is comparing Isaac and Ishmael to the law and faith? As Christians we aren't under the bondage of the law, but we are free through faith in Jesus Christ. Look at this Scripture in Romans 4:13-16

13 For the promise, that he should be the heir of the world, was not to Abraham, or to his seed, through the law, but through the righteousness of faith.
14 For if they which are of the law be heirs, faith is made void, and the promise made of none effect:

15 Because the law worketh wrath: for where no law is, there is no transgression.
16 Therefore it is of faith, that it might be by grace; to the end the promise might be sure to all the seed; not to that only which is of the law, but to that also which is of the faith of Abraham; who is the father of us all,

Daily Bible Scripture:

Galatians 4:21-31

21 Tell me, ye that desire to be under the law, do ye not hear the law?

22 For it is written, that Abraham had two sons, the one by a bondmaid, the other by a freewoman.

23 But he who was of the bondwoman was born after the flesh; but he of the freewoman was by promise.

24 Which things are an allegory: for these are the two covenants; the one from the mount Sinai, which gendereth to bondage, which is Agar.

25 For this Agar is mount Sinai in Arabia, and answereth to Jerusalem which now is, and is in bondage with her children.

26 But Jerusalem which is above is free, which is the mother of us all.

27 For it is written, Rejoice, thou barren that bearest not; break forth and cry, thou that travailest not: for the desolate hath many more children than she which hath an husband.

28 Now we, brethren, as Isaac was, are the children of promise.

29 But as then he that was born after the flesh persecuted him that was born after the Spirit, even so it is now.

30 Nevertheless what saith the scripture? Cast out the bondwoman and her son: for the son of the bondwoman shall not be heir with the son of the freewoman.

31 So then, brethren, we are not children of the bondwoman, but of the free.

Things to think about:

Why would anyone prefer to live under the law or by grace? Do you have a preference?

Why do we try to put ourselves back under the law when Jesus died to set us free from the law?

What does it mean to be children of the promise?

What does it mean to you to live free from bondage?

Prayer of the Day:

Dear Heavenly Father,

We thank You for this Scripture in the book of Galatians where Paul explains to the Galatians about the difference of living in bondage and being free. Help us to accept the free gift of salvation through Your Son, Jesus. Help us to keep ourselves out of bondage, and live in grace and faith. Thank You for loving us and giving us this special gift of freedom. In Jesus' precious name, we pray. Amen.

Stand Fast
Lesson 13
Galatians 5:15

As we continue with Paul's letter to the Galatians, Paul tells them to stand fast in the liberty and freedom of Christ and warns them not to get entangled with the yoke of bondage. Don't mistake this freedom of Christ to mean you can go out and do whatever you want. That's not what it means.

The freedom we have in Christ is freedom from sin. The freedom Christ died for was to cover our sins on the cross so we didn't have to try to earn our way to God by trying to perfectly follow all the rules and regulations of the Old Testament. Even though Christ died on the cross to free us from sin, a lot of people still live under bondage trying to earn their way to Christ by thinking they are good or by trying to do good things.

Those who live in the Spirit wait for the hope of righteousness by faith. In Jesus Christ it doesn't matter whether you are circumcised or not. It is faith that works love. Paul reminds the Galatians that they were running well, and asks who hindered them and caused them not to obey the truth? Paul knew they had been persuaded by someone other than the one who first called them to faith in Christ.

Paul says a little leaven leavens the whole lump. Leaven is yeast, which makes bread rise. You only have to put a little bit of yeast in bread to make the whole batch rise. It's kind of like saying one bad apple spoils the whole barrel. When you get wrong doctrine, or sin, in a body of believers it will eventually spoil the whole group.

Paul tells them he has confidence in them in the Lord, that they will be like-minded. Paul declares that whoever is trying to influence them otherwise will be judged by God. Paul's desire was those who were causing this trouble in the churches of Galatia to be cut off from them.

Paul asked them if he was still preaching circumcision or the law, then why was he being persecuted. He reminds them if they were going to follow the law they have to follow the whole law; they can't just pick and choose what parts they want to follow, in order to feel like they were good enough to get to heaven. If we were justified by the law, we would be fallen from grace.

Christ died on the cross to free us from the bondage of living under the law. Why would we want to go back to living under the law, when we can be free?

Paul tells them they have been called to liberty; however, they aren't to use that liberty to satisfy the flesh. He encourages them to serve one another in love. He says, all the law is fulfilled in this one statement, "Thou shall love thy neighbor as thyself."

Paul warns them if they fight and devour one another, to be careful that they aren't consumed of one another. It isn't good for us to be having disagreements among the body of Christ. We're to come together in one mind, loving one another, and serving one another as Christ loved us and gave Himself for us.

Daily Bible Scripture:

Galatians 5:1-15

1 Stand fast therefore in the liberty wherewith Christ hath made us free, and be not entangled again with the yoke of bondage.

2 Behold, I Paul say unto you, that if ye be circumcised, Christ shall profit you nothing.

3 For I testify again to every man that is circumcised, that he is a debtor to do the whole law.

4 Christ is become of no effect unto you, whosoever of you are justified by the law; ye are fallen from grace.

5 For we through the Spirit wait for the hope of righteousness by faith.

6 For in Jesus Christ neither circumcision availeth any thing, nor uncircumcision; but faith which worketh by love.

7 Ye did run well; who did hinder you that ye should not obey the truth?

8 This persuasion cometh not of him that calleth you.

9 A little leaven leaveneth the whole lump.

10 I have confidence in you through the Lord, that ye will be none otherwise minded: but he that troubleth you shall bear his judgment, whosoever he be.

11 And I, brethren, if I yet preach circumcision, why do I yet suffer

persecution? then is the offence of the cross ceased.

12 I would they were even cut off which trouble you.

13 For, brethren, ye have been called unto liberty; only [use] not liberty for an occasion to the flesh, but by love serve one another.

14 For all the law is fulfilled in one word, even in this; Thou shalt love thy neighbour as thyself.

15 But if ye bite and devour one another, take heed that ye be not consumed one of another.

Things to think about:

What does it mean to live under the law?

What does it mean to live by grace through faith?

Are you living in the liberty Christ died to give you? If not, why? If so, how?

Prayer of the Day:

Dear Heavenly Father,

Thank You for this Scripture in the book of Galatians where Paul talks to the Galatians about not being influenced by people who are trying to put them back in bondage under the law. Help us to accept the blessing that was given to us through Jesus Christ. Forgive us of the times we've tried to earn our way to You, knowing full well we would never be able to. We pray that You would convict the hearts and call those who haven't already accepted Jesus as their Savior. In Jesus' name, we pray. Amen.

Walk in the Spirit
Lesson 14
Galatians 5:16-26

Paul continues with his letter to the churches at Galatia instructing them to walk in the Spirit so they won't fulfill the lust of the flesh. Do you know what Paul means by telling them to walk in the Spirit?

When Paul speaks of the Spirit, he is talking about the Holy Spirit, the third person of the trinity. God is made up of three parts - God, the Father, God, the Son, and God, the Holy Spirit. When a person gets saved, or accepts Jesus as their Savior, the Holy Spirit comes to live within the new believer. He helps to lead, guide, and direct him to do the right thing in his life. He also comforts the believer.

The flesh (our earthly body) lusts against the Spirit, and the Spirit against the flesh. The flesh and the Spirit oppose one another, which causes us not to be able to do the things that we know are right sometimes. It is like a war is going on inside of us. It is the war against good and evil. If you are led of the Spirit, you aren't under the law.

Paul includes a long list of sins that are manifest in the body, in Galatians 5:19-21, when you turn your will over to the desires of the flesh, by listening to and giving into the temptation to do wrong. Paul says those who practice these things won't inherit the kingdom of God.

In Romans 7 Paul talks about the "inward man," which is the "Spiritual man" and the "outward man," which is the "flesh" and how there is a battle that goes on between the two of them. He talks about how sometimes we know that we should do good, but we don't do it.

In this Scripture in John, Jesus Himself is talking to Nicodemus and tells him "You must be born again." John 3:5-7:

5 Jesus answered, Verily, verily, I say unto thee, Except a man be born of water and of the Spirit, he cannot enter into the kingdom of God.

6 That which is born of the flesh is flesh; and that which is born of the Spirit is spirit.

7 Marvel not that I said unto thee, Ye must be born again.

When we are born into this world of our mother we are born of water and of the flesh. Since the fall of Adam every person who is born of the flesh is born in sin. To be born of the Spirit you have to accept Jesus as your Savior, and then the Spirit comes and abides with you.

In this Scripture, Paul talks next about the fruits of the Spirit, which are love, joy, peace, longsuffering, gentleness goodness, faith, meekness, and temperance. These are the characteristics that a Christian living in the Spirit should have. Paul says that those who belong to Christ have crucified the flesh, including its affections and the lusts of the flesh. Look at these two sets of characteristics and see where they fit into your life.

Romans 8:1 says, "There is therefore now no condemnation to them which are in Christ Jesus, who walk not after the flesh, but after the Spirit." Once you become a Christian all the sins you have committed are covered by Jesus' blood through His death on the cross. He took the punishment for our sins.

If you are a Christian, does that mean you will always do the right thing or act the right way? No, it doesn't, because we still have the flesh - our earthly desires and temptations - to deal with in this life. The more you study God's Word and develop a closer relationship with Him the more you will see the Spirit at work in your life. Paul says, "If we live in the Spirit, let us also walk in the Spirit." Not desiring vain glory, provoking one another or being envious of one another.

Daily Bible Scripture:

Galatians 5:16-26

16 This I say then, Walk in the Spirit, and ye shall not fulfil the lust of the flesh.

17 For the flesh lusteth against the Spirit, and the Spirit against the flesh: and these are contrary the one to the other: so that ye cannot do the things that ye would.

18 But if ye be led of the Spirit, ye are not under the law.

19 Now the works of the flesh are manifest, which are these; Adultery,

fornication, uncleanness, lasciviousness,

20 Idolatry, witchcraft, hatred, variance, emulations, wrath, strife, seditions, heresies,

21 Envyings, murders, drunkenness, revellings, and such like: of the which I tell you before, as I have also told you in time past, that they which do such things shall not inherit the kingdom of God.

22 But the fruit of the Spirit is love, joy, peace, longsuffering, gentleness, goodness, faith,

23 Meekness, temperance: against such there is no law.

24 And they that are Christ's have crucified the flesh with the affections and lusts.

25 If we live in the Spirit, let us also walk in the Spirit.

26 Let us not be desirous of vain glory, provoking one another, envying one another.

Things to think about:

What are considered to be the works of the flesh?

What are the fruits of the Spirit?

In what ways are you walking in the Spirit?

Prayer of the Day:

Dear Heavenly Father,

Thank You for this Scripture in the book of Galatians where Paul talks about the difference between walking in the Spirit and walking in the flesh. Help us to always follow the Spirit in our lives. Forgive us of the times we have let the flesh rule in our lives. Give us strength day to day to do Your will. Help us to have the fruit of the Spirit alive and working in our lives. In Jesus' name, we pray. Amen.

Bear One Another's Burdens
Lesson 15
Galatians 6:1-9

As we continue in the book of Galatians with Paul's letter to the churches of Galatia, Paul exhorts the brethren who are spiritual to restore anyone who is overtaken in a fault, with meekness; for fear that they may also be tempted. What do you think Paul means by this?

Paul tells them to bear one another's burdens so that they may fulfill the law of Christ. Paul may be saying to them, "Instead of imposing the law as a burden upon your fellow Christians, you should lift their burdens by restoring them to fellowship with Jesus Christ, thus fulfilling Christ's law."

As Christians we aren't to judge one another, but we are to support, encourage, and uplift one another. Paul warns the Galatians about being judgmental and tells them to treat each other with gentleness. Today, we can't be prideful, because we too could be tempted. Everybody makes mistakes from time to time. Paul is not talking about someone who habitually chooses to sin. He is talking about someone who is overtaken by sin, and repents sincerely desiring not to commit the sin again.

Rather than criticizing someone and tearing them down even further with gossip, Paul says we're to restore them. We don't need to ignore sin and act like it didn't happen, but we need to help them to recover from their sin. We need to pray for them and lift them up to God rather than gossiping about their faults.

Paul says that if a man thinks himself to be something when he is nothing he deceives himself. The Bible says that we have all sinned and come short of the glory of God (Romans 3:23) and that none of us are righteous (Romans 3:10).

Let every man prove his own work, and then he can celebrate in himself alone and not in another. Every man has to bear his own burden. In this life we all have burdens to bear. Some of them other people can help us with, and some of them we have to work through ourselves, with the help of God.

Those who are trained in the Word are to communicate with those who teach in all good things. Paul warns the Galatians not to be deceived, because God is not mocked, whatever we sow we will reap. If you sow to the flesh you will reap corruption, but if you sow to the Spirit you will reap life everlasting. Paul says to not get weary in doing well, we will reap in due season if we don't faint.

If we do things that are wrong we will suffer the consequences. There are always consequences for the decisions we make. If we make right choices there will be rewards for them as well.

I exhort you to do as this Scripture says and fight the good fight of faith: 1 Timothy 6:12, "Fight the good fight of faith, lay hold on eternal life, whereunto thou art also called, and hast professed a good profession before many witnesses."

Daily Bible Scripture:

Galatians 6:1-9

1 Brethren, if a man be overtaken in a fault, ye which are spiritual, restore such an one in the spirit of meekness; considering thyself, lest thou also be tempted.

2 Bear ye one another's burdens, and so fulfil the law of Christ.

3 For if a man think himself to be something, when he is nothing, he deceiveth himself.

4 But let every man prove his own work, and then shall he have rejoicing in himself alone, and not in another.

5 For every man shall bear his own burden.

6 Let him that is taught in the word communicate unto him that teacheth in all good things.

7 Be not deceived; God is not mocked: for whatsoever a man soweth, that shall he also reap.

8 For he that soweth to his flesh shall of the flesh reap corruption; but he that soweth to the Spirit shall of the Spirit reap life everlasting.

9 And let us not be weary in well doing: for in due season we shall reap, if we faint not.

Things to think about:

How does Paul advise us to handle a brother who is overtaken by sin?

What does Paul say about sowing and reaping?

What is the difference in sowing to the flesh or to the Spirit?

Prayer of the Day:

Dear Heavenly Father,

Thank You for this Scripture in the book of Galatians where Paul says to restore those who have fallen. Help us to be humble when dealing with such a situation. Give us wisdom in knowing how to handle these kinds of things. Help us to sow to the Spirit so we can reap life everlasting. Give us strength to fight the good fight of faith. In Jesus' name, we pray. Amen.

Do Good to All Men
Lesson 16
Galatians 6:10-18

In this portion of the letter Paul says we are to do good to all men—meaning all people, especially those who are of the household of faith. Why do you think Paul gives this advice?

Paul tells them, "You see how large a letter I have written to you with my own hand?" Paul's love and concern for the Galatians is shown throughout this letter. His main concern is that the people of Galatia had been influenced to return to following the Law of Moses in order to be Christians. Paul knew that Jesus died on the cross so they could be free from the law. He wanted the Galatians to live in the freedom Christ died to give them.

Paul says there are many who desire to make a show in the flesh by compelling them to be circumcised, one of the Jewish laws. Remember, those other teachers were only trying to persuade them to do this so they can glory in their flesh, bragging that they had persuaded more people to follow the Jewish traditions. Paul says, God forbid that I should glory except in the cross of Christ, by who the world is crucified to me, and I to the world. Paul didn't want any glory for what he did. His ministry was for Christ and any good that came of it the glory went to Christ.

Paul says, "In Christ neither circumcision (following Jewish laws) nor un-circumcision (boasting in freedom from Jewish laws) gains anything, but we are made new creatures in Christ. As many of you as walk according to this rule, may God's peace and mercy be on you and on the Israel of God." Paul says from now on do not let anybody bother me, because I have in my body the marks of the Lord Jesus.

Perhaps Paul thought, if you want to be circumcised, go ahead and do that, but do it for the right reasons. If you follow the other laws make sure you do it as a sign of your faith, not as a sign of your own righteousness. Sure I was circumcised, but that was before I became a Christian, while I called myself a Jew. Maybe Paul wouldn't have chosen to be circumcised if he'd become a Christian first (even though in today's world many baby boys are circumcised before they leave the hospital to come home).

Paul had suffered much persecution over the years for his stand for Christ. It had taken its toll on his body. The burden that pastors, teachers, and leaders have on their hearts for the people is heavy. Paul loved the Galatians and wanted God's best for them. Paul closes the letter saying, "The grace of our Lord Jesus Christ be with your spirit." Perhaps, a common benediction used in many churches today.

Paul had served the Galatians and he had a heart for them. His desire for them was that they continue in the work of the Lord which he had taught them. He wanted them to have the joy and peace of salvation through Jesus Christ. He didn't want them to go back to being a slave to the law and being in bondage. Christ died for our sins so we could have grace, peace, and forgiveness and be free from the bondage of the law. Why would we want to be entrapped in that bondage if we don't have to be?

Daily Bible Scripture:

Galatians 6:10-18

10 As we have therefore opportunity, let us do good unto all men, especially unto them who are of the household of faith.

11 Ye see how large a letter I have written unto you with mine own hand.

12 As many as desire to make a fair shew in the flesh, they constrain you to be circumcised; only lest they should suffer persecution for the cross of Christ.

13 For neither they themselves who are circumcised keep the law; but desire to have you circumcised, that they may glory in your flesh.

14 But God forbid that I should glory, save in the cross of our Lord Jesus Christ, by whom the world is crucified unto me, and I unto the world.

15 For in Christ Jesus neither circumcision availeth any thing, nor uncircumcision, but a new creature.

16 And as many as walk according to this rule, peace be on them, and mercy, and upon the Israel of God.

17 From henceforth let no man trouble me: for I bear in my body the marks of the Lord Jesus.

18 Brethren, the grace of our Lord Jesus Christ be with your spirit. Amen.

[[[The following was added by editors of the KJV: To [the] Galatians written from Rome.]]]

Things to think about:

Why did Paul exhort the Galatians to do good to those who were of the household of faith?

What did Paul glory in?

Have you been set free through Jesus Christ?

Prayer of the Day:

Dear Heavenly Father,

Thank You for this Scripture in the book of Galatians where we've studied Paul's letter to the Galatians. We thank You that Paul has repeatedly explained how we can have the freedom of Christ in our lives. Thank You that we don't have to live under the bondage of the law anymore. Thank You for the precious gift You gave us through Your Son, Jesus Christ. Help us to treasure Him and the gift of salvation. In Jesus' precious name, we pray. Amen.